BATMAN™

DARK KNIGHT ACTIVITIES

TIME
4:30

INC: PXS
TAR: 4E14
CLAS: VOJ-TA

RNG: 14.6

PaRragon

Bath • New York • Cologne • Melbourne • Delhi
Hong Kong • Shenzhen • Singapore

This edition published by Parragon Books Ltd in 2016

Parragon Books Ltd
Chartist House
15–17 Trim Street
Bath BA1 1HA, UK
www.parragon.com
Please retain this information for future reference.

ISBN 978-1-4748-5117-6

Printed in China

BATMAN NAME GAME

Unleash Batman's awesome nicknames by using the words in the green box to fill in the blanks.

CRUSADER
DETECTIVE
DARK

WORLD'S GREATEST _ _ _ _ _ _ _ _ _

THE _ _ _ _ KNIGHT

THE CAPED _ _ _ _ _ _ _ _

Now think of your own awesome name for Batman:

DID YOU KNOW?
Batman is a member of an elite team of super heroes known as the Justice League.

Answers on page 48

TURBO SUDOKU

Batman always travels in style. Complete this picture
puzzle by writing the correct letters in the spaces.
Each row and column should contain one of each picture.

SIGNAL FAILURE

Police Commissioner Gordon needs Batman's help, but the Bat-Signal has pieces missing! Can you draw lines to match the pieces to the gaps?

ENEMY ALERT!

These are some of Batman's most hair-raising foes. Unscramble their names and write them at the bottom of the page.

1. TOW-FCAE

2. EHT RELDDIR

3. TEH KERJO

4. HET EGNIPUN

5. NMA-TBA

1. ....   2. ....

3. ....   4. ....

5. ....

   Answers on page 48

ROBIN TO THE RESCUE

With so many super-villains on the loose, the Dark Knight can never rest. Thank goodness he has a crime-fighting partner to help him out. Only two of these pictures of Robin are the same. Can you spot the matching pair?

ANSWER:

Answer on page 48

FIGHT KNIGHT

BAM! Batman is about to unleash a powerful punch – but who's on the receiving end? Draw a villain on the opposite page, then colour in your picture.

WORD ATTACK

Look closely at the words on this page.
Can you spot what they have in common?
Write your answer in the box.

combat

bath

debate

battery

baton

acrobat

ANSWER:

BATMAN JIGSAW

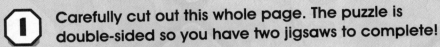

Follow these three easy steps to make a double-sided jigsaw:

1 Carefully cut out this whole page. The puzzle is double-sided so you have two jigsaws to complete!

2 Cut along the dotted lines below to create your puzzle pieces.

3 Mix up the pieces. Now try to put the pictures back together. Complete one picture and then try the other.

WHAT COMES NEXT?

The Dark Knight is in his Batcave trying out some new fight moves! Look carefully at each sequence and then decide which picture should come next. Write the correct letter at the end of each row.

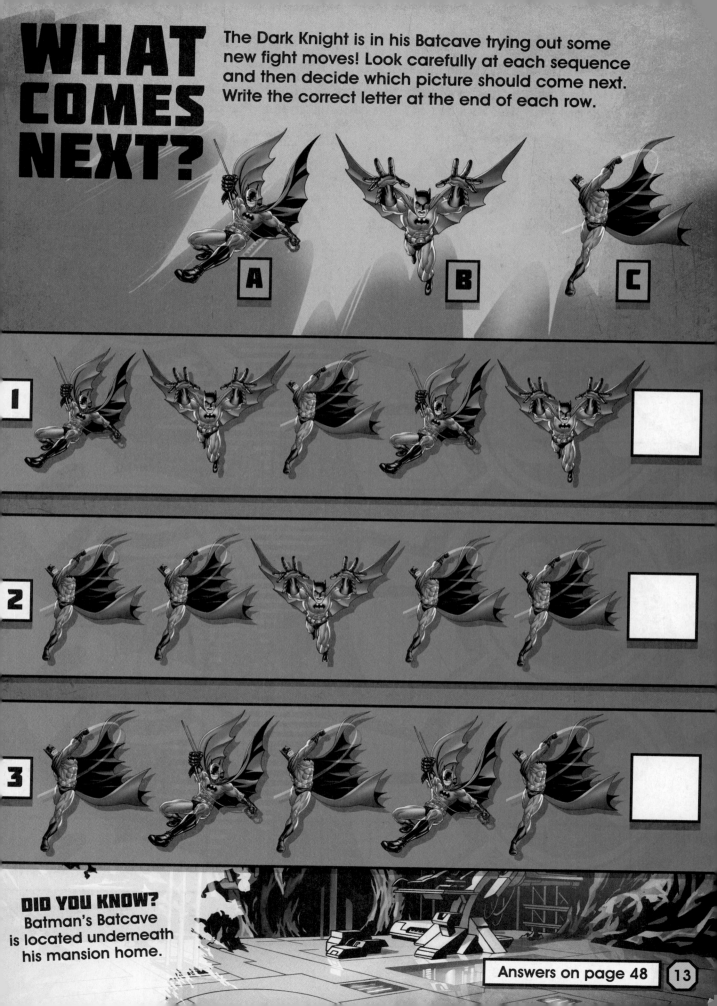

DID YOU KNOW?
Batman's Batcave is located underneath his mansion home.

Answers on page 48

CLOSE ENCOUNTERS

Batman is doing some important detective work but the zoom lens on his camera is faulty.
Can you work out who he's looking at? The green panel at the bottom will help you.

1

2

3

4

TWO-FACE   ROBIN   THE RIDDLER   THE JOKER

FIGHTING TALK

Complete these comics with awesome sound effects! Choose from the suggestions below or create your own.

POW! THWACK!
BAM! FWOOSHH!
THUMP! THWAAAP!
BOOM! KLANG!

EMAIL ENIGMA

Batman has received a mysterious encrypted email. Can you help him decode it? For every letter, write down the letter that comes next in the alphabet.

Tip: If the coded letter is Z, go back to the start of the alphabet.

FNSGZL HM SQNTAKD, GTQQX!

— — — — — — — —

— — — — — — — '

— — — — !

Answer on page 48

WORD DETECTIVE

How many Batman words from the list below can you find in the grid? Look left to right and up and down.

D	E	T	E	C	T	I	V	E
C	E	S	K	P	G	A	H	C
R	G	O	T	H	A	M	R	R
K	N	I	G	H	T	K	N	U
C	E	H	K	E	S	K	E	S
M	A	C	G	K	M	D	N	A
A	B	A	D	I	M	G	G	D
S	L	P	E	F	N	L	H	E
K	C	E	M	A	A	K	E	R

KNIGHT **GOTHAM**

CAPE **DETECTIVE**

MASK **CRUSADER**

Answers on page 48

BATTLE
FOR GOTHAM CITY

Gotham City is under attack from the Joker and his friends. Help Batman reach a building that's under attack, avoiding the bad guys along the way.

START

FINISH

COUNT THE BATARANGS

How many times does Batman's Batarang appear on this page?

Answer on page 48

FIND THE THIEF

Which of these villains stole Batman's Batcycle?
Use the clues at the bottom of the page to find the thief.

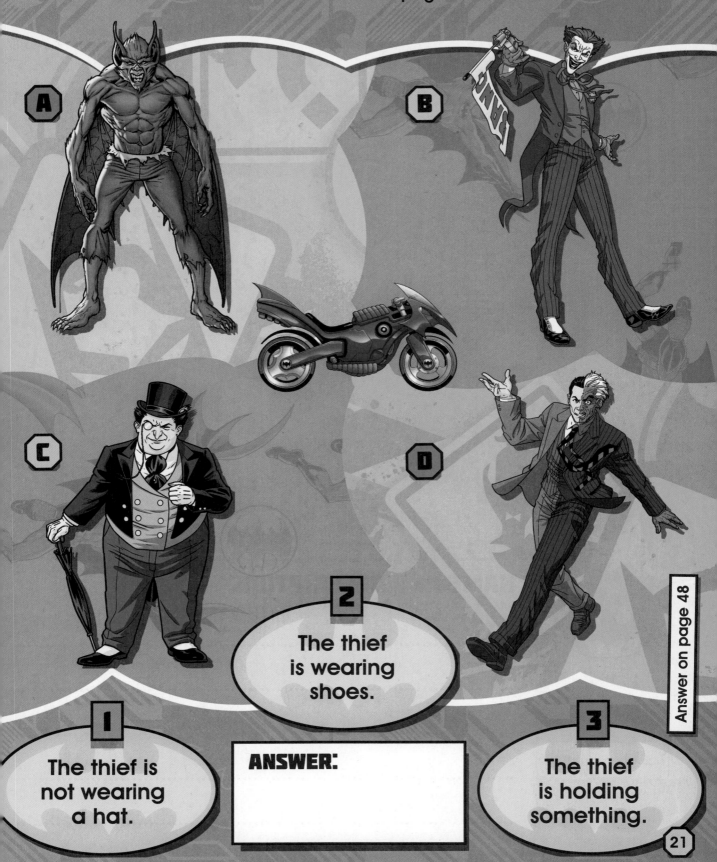

A

B

C

D

2

The thief is wearing shoes.

1

The thief is not wearing a hat.

ANSWER:

3

The thief is holding something.

Answer on page 48

21

DESIGN A GADGET

Create a new gadget for Batman's hi-tech collection.
Draw your idea in the space below and then explain
how it works. Don't forget to give it a cool name, too.

BATMAN'S NEW GADGET!

NAME AND DESCRIPTION:

....

....

....

....

....

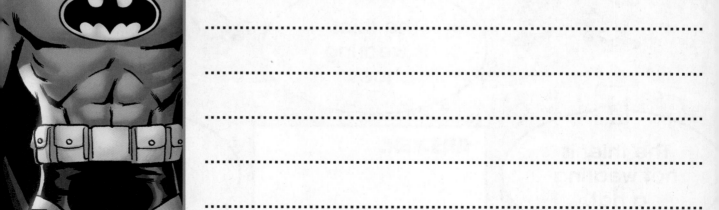

BRAIN STRAIN

How many words can you make using the letters in
'Caped Crusader'?
The first one has been done for you.

read

MULTIPLE MAYHEM

Batman is going through his surveillance photographs.
Can you count how many times each super-villain appears
in these pictures? Write the numbers in the circles below.

Answers on page 48

 The Joker = ◯

 The Riddler = ◯

 Man-Bat = ◯

 Two-Face = ◯

DARKNESS FALLS

There's been a power cut in Gotham City! Can you identify these Justice League members by their shadowy shapes? Write the correct letters in the circles at the bottom of the page.

Superman = ◯   Batman = ◯   The Flash = ◯   Green Lantern = ◯

THE RIDDLER'S RIDICULOUS RIDDLES

Help the Dark Knight by working out these baffling brainteasers. We've listed the answers to help you. Write the correct letter underneath each riddle.

1 What has a face and two hands but no arms or legs?

....

2 Which month has 28 days?

....

3 What goes up and doesn't come back down?

....

4 What begins with T, ends with T, and has T in it?

....

Answers on page 48

ANSWERS

A All of them

B Your age

C A clock

D A teapot

DID YOU KNOW?

The Riddler isn't obsessed only with riddles. He loves puzzles and word games, too.

MIND OVER MATTER

It's time for a memory test! Look carefully at this page for 30 seconds. Now cover up the page and use a separate piece of paper to write down as many Batman items as you can remember. How did you do?

BATCYCLE

BATARANG

SWORD

BAT-SYMBOL

BATMOBILE

NIGHT WATCHMAN

Batman is keeping watch from the rooftops of Gotham City. Can you spot where each of the five close-ups appear in the scene?

BONUS BATARANGS

Can you spot four Batarangs in the scene?

Answers on page 48

FINISH THE VILLAIN

Using the left-hand grid as a guide, copy the evil side of Harvey Two-Face into the right-hand grid. Now colour in your picture!

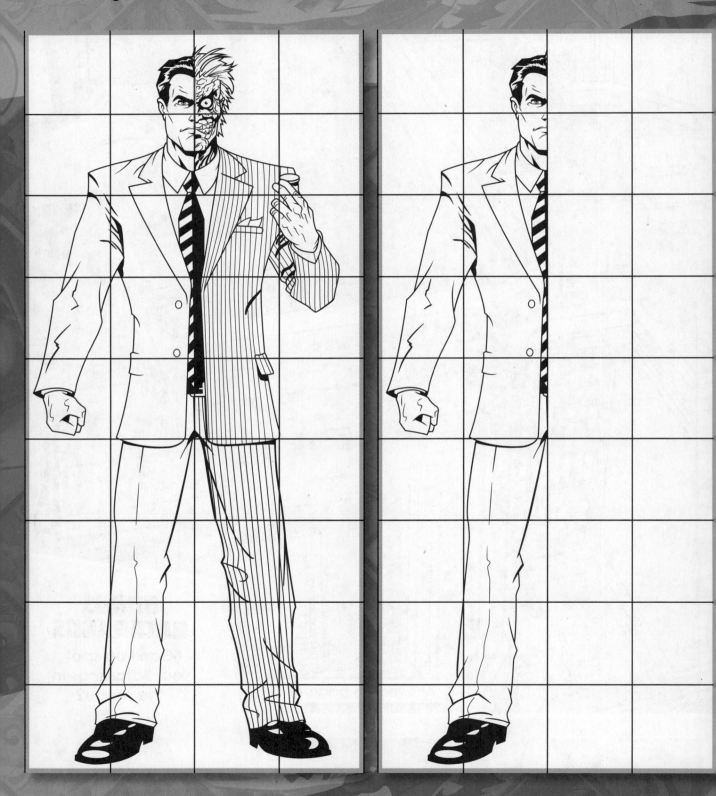

CHOOSE YOUR SUPER-HERO NAME

Follow the steps below to discover your super-hero name!

Count the letters in your first name. Now use this number to find the first part of your super-hero name:

- 2 = AMAZING
- 3 = FANTASTIC
- 4 = HUMONGOUS
- 5 = ORANGE
- 6 = ANGRY
- 7 = PROFESSOR
- 8 = FIERY
- 9 = INVINCIBLE
- 10 = HUMAN
- 11 = SUPER

Now use the month of your birthday to find the second part:

- January = GIRL/BOY
- February = INFERNO
- March = SNOWBALL
- April = ATOM
- May = NEWT
- June = TORNADO
- July = ANDROID
- August = HURRICANE
- September = WOLF
- October = BEAST
- November = EAGLE
- December = ROCK

MY SUPER-HERO NAME IS:

GOTHAM CITY'S PROTECTOR

Batman is racing to the rescue! Can you spot six differences in the bottom picture? Colour in a Batcycle for every difference you find.

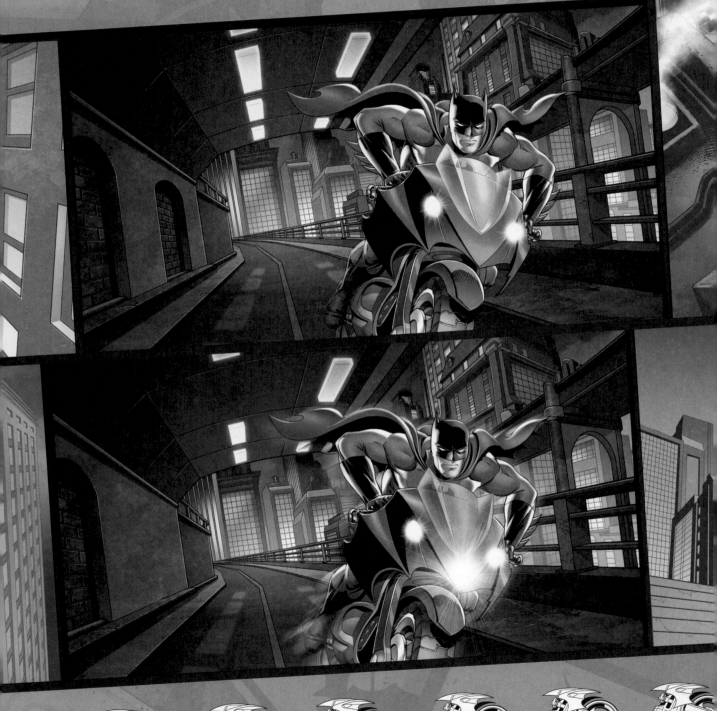

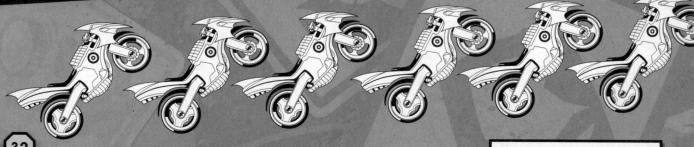

Answers on page 48

PATH TO VICTORY

Batman is fighting Man-Bat, but he could do with some extra help. Which path will lead the Dark Knight to his Batarang?

DID YOU KNOW?

Man-Bat used to be a scientist called Dr Kirk Langstrom. He tested a formula on himself, but something went wrong and he turned into the bat-like monster!

Answer on page 48

"I'M BATMAN!"

A hero! An enigma!
Can you think of six more words
to describe Batman that start
with the letters in his name?

B

A

T

M

A

N

CRISIS POINT

Two-Face is threatening the Justice League headquarters! Help Batman reach the control centre by following the numbers in order from 1 to 20 through the grid. Move up, down, left or right – not diagonally.

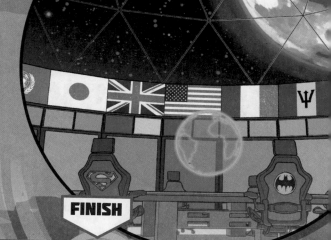

FINISH

11	17	12	5	17	20	11	18
5	11	16	17	18	19	2	17
8	2	15	14	2	5	18	14
3	5	9	13	12	11	10	9
			15	12	5	16	8
			2	4	5	6	7
			13	3	2	19	17
			1	2	7	18	16

START

Answer on page 48

BEHIND THE MASK!

Did you know Batman has a secret identity? Circle every second letter to reveal the name of Batman's billionaire alias. We've done the first one for you.

START ▶ K B A R E U C C P E G M W C A L Y A N M E

Batman's alias is:

B _ _ _ _ _   _ _ _ _ _

HERO POSTER

Add some cool colours to this awesome Batman poster!

HIDE AND PEEK

Gotham City is a dangerous place – there's a villain lurking around every corner. Look closely at this picture. Can you spot the Joker, Two-Face and the Riddler?

Answers on page 48

PICK OUT THE PENGUIN

Which of these pictures of the Penguin is different from the rest?
Put a tick next to your answer.

A

B

C

D

E

F

DID YOU KNOW?
The Penguin's real name is Oswald Chesterfield Cobblepot!

Answer on page 48

MASTER OF MARTIAL ARTS

Which of Batman's moves is strongest? Add up the numbers in the white stars next to each move. The one with the highest number is the winner.

LETHAL LEAP — 2, 3, 1

FOOT SMASH — 5, 1, 1

FIST POUND — 3, 3, 2

THE WINNING MOVE IS:

Answer on page 48

BATMOBILE BREAK-UP

Help the Caped Crusader piece his Batmobile back together.
Write the letters in the correct order under the bottom picture.

A B C D E F G H I J

Answer on page 48

FEARLESS FUNNIES

The Joker loves telling jokes – especially when they're about Batman. Giggle at these and then try them out on your friends.

Why did the Dark Knight's date go badly?

He had 'bat' breath.

How does Alfred call the Caped Crusader to dinner?

Dinner, dinner, dinner, dinner BATMAN!

Why couldn't Batman go fishing?

Because Robin ate all the worms.

What is Batman's favourite part of a joke?

The 'punch' line.

What does Alfred say to Batman when he goes to bed?

Night, Knight!

What do you get if you cross Batman with a steamroller?

Flatman!

HA HA

RESCUE MISSION

Oh no, Robin is trapped! Guide Batman through the maze so he can free his friend.

START

Answer on page 48

COMPLETE THE CAPE

Finish this picture of Batman by joining the dots, and then colour it in.

Batman is the world's greatest detective. He sees everything and misses nothing. Can the same be said about you? Let's find out....

1. Batman is also known as:

   a) Man-Bat

   b) The Caped Crusader

   c) The Caped Knight

2. Batman's alias is:

   a) Bruce Wayne

   b) Wayne Bruce

   c) Clark Kent

3. Batman's butler is called:

   a) Carson

   b) Jeeves

   c) Alfred

4. Batman is a member of the:

   a) Justice League

   b) Defence League

   c) Super Hero League

Answers on page 48

ANSWERS

Page 3
World's Greatest Detective
The Dark Knight
The Caped Crusader

Page 4

Page 5

Page 6
1. Two-Face
2. The Riddler
3. The Joker
4. The Penguin
5. Man-Bat

Page 7
A and D are identical

Page 10
All the words include
the word 'bat'

Page 13
1. C, 2. B, 3. A

Page 14
1. The Joker
2. Robin
3. The Riddler
4. Two-Face

Page 16
Gotham In
trouble, hurry!

Page 17

D	E	T	E	C	T	I	V	E
C	E	S	K	P	G	A	H	C
R	G	O	T	H	A	M	R	R
K	N	I	G	H	T	K	N	U
C	E	H	K	E	S	K	E	S
M	A	C	G	K	M	D	N	A
A	B	A	D	V	M	G	G	D
S	L	P	E	F	B	L	H	E
K	C	E	M	A	A	K	E	R

Pages 18–19

Page 20
The Batarang appears
16 times

Page 21
B. The Joker

Page 24
The Joker = 6
The Riddler = 4
Man-Bat = 1
Two-Face = 2

Page 25
Superman = B
Batman = D
The Flash = C
Green Lantern = A

Page 26
1. C, 2. A,
3. B, 4. D

Pages 28–29

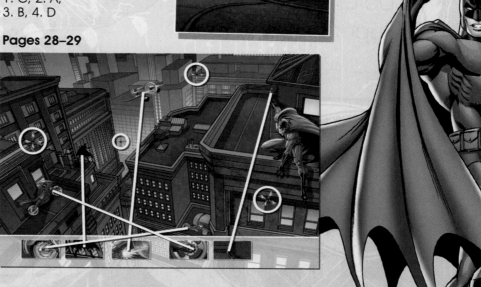

Page 32

Page 33
Path C

Page 35

11	17	12	5	17	20	11	18
5	11	16	17	18	19	2	17
8	2	15	14	2	5	18	14
3	5	9	13	12	11	10	9
			15	12	5	16	8
			2	4	5	2	7
			13	3	2	19	17
			1	2	7	18	16

Page 36
Bruce Wayne

Page 40

Page 41
D is the odd one out

Page 42
Fist pound is the winner

Page 43
H, G, C, F, J, D, B, A, I, E

Page 45

Page 47
1. b) The Caped Crusader
2. a) Bruce Wayne
3. c) Alfred
4. a) Justice League